EMMANUEL JOSEPH

The Unfolding Hourglass, Time, Growth, and the Art of Living Fully

Copyright © 2025 by Emmanuel Joseph

All rights reserved. No part of this publication may be reproduced, stored or transmitted in any form or by any means, electronic, mechanical, photocopying, recording, scanning, or otherwise without written permission from the publisher. It is illegal to copy this book, post it to a website, or distribute it by any other means without permission.

First edition

This book was professionally typeset on Reedsy. Find out more at reedsy.com

Contents

1	Chapter 1: Embracing the Moment	1
2	Chapter 2: The Tapestry of Time	3
3	Chapter 3: The Dance of Growth	5
4	Chapter 4: The Art of Mindfulness	7
5	Chapter 5: The Wisdom of Impermanence	9
6	Chapter 6: The Power of Connection	11
7	Chapter 7: The Journey Within	13
8	Chapter 8: The Balance of Being and Doing	15
9	Chapter 9: The Flow of Creativity	17
10	Chapter 10: The Gift of Gratitude	19
11	Chapter 11: The Courage to Change	21
12	Chapter 12: The Joy of Simplicity	23
13	Chapter 13: The Strength of Vulnerability	25
14	Chapter 14: The Power of Purpose	27
15	Chapter 15: The Beauty of Compassion	29
16	Chapter 16: The Harmony of Balance	31
17	Chapter 17: The Legacy of a Life Fully Lived	33

1

Chapter 1: Embracing the Moment

In the ceaseless flow of time, every moment we encounter is a gift, an ephemeral speck of existence that invites us to savor its essence. Each breath we take, every sunrise we witness, and every smile we share encapsulates the transient beauty of life. To embrace the moment is to acknowledge its impermanence, to find joy in its fleeting nature, and to live with the awareness that today will soon become a memory. We often rush through our days, caught in the whirlwind of routines and responsibilities, forgetting to pause and appreciate the subtle wonders that surround us. The art of living fully begins with the simple act of being present, of immersing ourselves in the here and now, and cherishing the uniqueness of each passing second.

Being present is not just about physical presence; it is about engaging our minds, hearts, and souls in the current moment. It is about listening intently when someone speaks, truly tasting our food, feeling the warmth of the sun on our skin, and noticing the small details that make life extraordinary. By practicing mindfulness and gratitude, we can transform ordinary moments into extraordinary experiences. When we learn to embrace the moment, we open ourselves to the richness of life and cultivate a deeper sense of fulfillment and joy.

Living in the moment also means letting go of the past and not worrying excessively about the future. It involves releasing regrets, forgiving ourselves and others, and finding peace in the present. The past has shaped who we are, but it does not define us. The future holds endless possibilities, but it is shaped by the choices we make today. By focusing on the present, we can make the most of our time and create a life that is meaningful and aligned with our values and aspirations.

In our fast-paced world, it can be challenging to slow down and be present. We are constantly bombarded with distractions and demands that pull us in different directions. However, by consciously choosing to embrace the moment, we can reclaim our time and live more intentionally. Whether through meditation, deep breathing exercises, or simply taking a few moments each day to reflect and be still, we can cultivate a practice of mindfulness that enhances our overall well-being and enriches our lives.

2

Chapter 2: The Tapestry of Time

Time is not a linear progression of seconds, minutes, and hours; it is a rich tapestry woven with the threads of our experiences, emotions, and connections. Each thread tells a story, each moment adds depth to the fabric of our lives. As we journey through time, we leave behind a trail of memories that shape who we are and how we perceive the world. The tapestry of time is a mosaic of triumphs and tribulations, joys and sorrows, dreams and realities. It is a testament to our resilience, our capacity to grow and evolve, and our ability to find meaning in the midst of life's complexities. To live fully is to embrace the entirety of this tapestry, to honor the past, celebrate the present, and look forward to the future with hope and curiosity.

Our individual tapestries are unique, but they are also interconnected with the tapestries of others. The people we meet, the relationships we build, and the communities we are a part of, all contribute to the richness and diversity of our life stories. Each connection adds a new thread to our tapestry, creating a complex and beautiful pattern that reflects the myriad ways in which we touch and are touched by the lives of others.

The tapestry of time is also shaped by the choices we make and the paths we choose to follow. Every decision, whether big or small, influences the direction of our lives and the experiences we encounter. By making conscious and intentional choices, we can weave a tapestry that reflects our true selves and aligns with our deepest values and aspirations. It is through this process of deliberate living that we can create a life of purpose and fulfillment.

As we reflect on the tapestry of time, it is important to recognize that it is always evolving. The threads of our past, present, and future are constantly being woven together, creating new patterns and possibilities. Embracing this dynamic and ever-changing nature of life allows us to remain open to new experiences and opportunities. It encourages us to stay curious, to keep learning and growing, and to continue weaving the intricate and beautiful tapestry that is our life.

3

Chapter 3: The Dance of Growth

Growth is a dance, a dynamic interplay of challenges and opportunities, failures and successes. It is a continuous process of self-discovery, learning, and transformation. Just as a dancer moves gracefully across the stage, adapting to the rhythm and flow of the music, we too must navigate the ever-changing landscape of life with grace and resilience. Growth requires us to step out of our comfort zones, to embrace uncertainty, and to confront our fears and limitations. It calls us to cultivate a mindset of curiosity and openness, to seek out new experiences and perspectives, and to learn from our mistakes and setbacks. The dance of growth is a celebration of our potential, a testament to our capacity for change and renewal, and a reminder that we are always in the process of becoming.

The journey of growth is often marked by moments of discomfort and uncertainty. It is during these times that we are stretched beyond our perceived limits and pushed to explore new possibilities. Embracing these challenges with a positive attitude and a willingness to learn can lead to profound personal transformation. Each obstacle we encounter becomes an opportunity to develop new skills, gain new insights, and build greater resilience. By viewing growth as a dance, we can approach it with a sense of fluidity and adaptability, allowing ourselves to move with the rhythm of life.

A key aspect of growth is the willingness to take risks and make mistakes.

Fear of failure can hold us back from pursuing our dreams and realizing our full potential. However, by reframing failure as a valuable learning experience, we can overcome our fears and take bold steps toward our goals. Each mistake we make provides us with valuable feedback and insights that can guide our future actions. The dance of growth is about embracing imperfection and recognizing that progress is often made through trial and error.

Ultimately, the dance of growth is a journey of self-discovery and self-expression. It is about uncovering our unique strengths and talents, and finding ways to share them with the world. By embracing the process of growth with an open heart and mind, we can create a life that is authentic, fulfilling, and aligned with our true selves. The dance of growth is a testament to our innate potential and a reminder that we are always evolving and becoming more of who we are meant to be.

4

Chapter 4: The Art of Mindfulness

Mindfulness is the art of paying attention, of being fully present and engaged in the moment. It is a practice that invites us to cultivate a deeper awareness of our thoughts, emotions, and sensations, and to approach our experiences with a sense of curiosity and non-judgment. Mindfulness teaches us to slow down, to breathe deeply, and to savor the simple pleasures of life. It encourages us to let go of the past, release our worries about the future, and focus on the here and now. By practicing mindfulness, we can develop a greater sense of clarity, calm, and balance, and create a more intentional and fulfilling life. The art of mindfulness is not about escaping reality, but about embracing it fully, with all its beauty and imperfections.

Mindfulness is rooted in the tradition of meditation, but it can be practiced in many different ways. Whether through formal meditation, mindful breathing, or simply bringing awareness to our daily activities, we can cultivate a sense of presence and connection to the present moment. Mindfulness helps us to become more attuned to our inner experiences, as well as to the world around us. It allows us to observe our thoughts and emotions without judgment, and to respond to them with greater compassion and understanding.

One of the key benefits of mindfulness is its ability to reduce stress and enhance our overall well-being. By focusing on the present moment, we can break free from the cycle of rumination and worry that often contributes to stress and anxiety. Mindfulness teaches us to approach challenges with a sense of equanimity and resilience, and to find peace in the midst of life's ups and downs. It also enhances our capacity for joy and gratitude, allowing us to fully appreciate the beauty and richness of our lives.

Incorporating mindfulness into our daily lives requires practice and commitment. It involves making a conscious effort to slow down, to be present, and to cultivate a non-judgmental attitude toward ourselves and our experiences. By making mindfulness a regular part of our routine, we can create a more balanced and harmonious life. The art of mindfulness is a powerful tool for personal growth and transformation, and a reminder that true fulfillment comes from being fully present in the here and now.

5

Chapter 5: The Wisdom of Impermanence

Impermanence is a fundamental truth of existence, a reminder that everything in life is subject to change and transformation. The seasons shift, the tides ebb and flow, and our lives are marked by a constant flux of beginnings and endings. Embracing the wisdom of impermanence allows us to appreciate the preciousness of each moment and to live with a greater sense of gratitude and presence. It teaches us to let go of our attachments and expectations, and to find peace in the ever-changing nature of life. By accepting the impermanent nature of existence, we can cultivate a deeper sense of resilience and adaptability, and learn to navigate life's challenges with grace and equanimity. The wisdom of impermanence is a powerful reminder that every moment is a gift, and that the only constant in life is change.

The concept of impermanence is often associated with feelings of loss and uncertainty, but it can also be a source of profound liberation. By recognizing that everything is temporary, we can release our attachment to material possessions, relationships, and outcomes. This frees us from the burden of clinging to what is ultimately beyond our control and allows us to find joy in the present moment. Impermanence teaches us to appreciate the beauty of the here and now, and to savor the experiences and connections that enrich our lives.

Impermanence also encourages us to live with intention and purpose. Knowing that our time is limited, we are motivated to make the most of each day and to prioritize what truly matters. It inspires us to be more present with our loved ones, to pursue our passions, and to contribute to the world in meaningful ways. The wisdom of impermanence reminds us that life is a precious and fleeting gift, and that we have the power to shape our own legacy through our actions and choices.

In embracing impermanence, we also cultivate a greater sense of compassion and empathy. Understanding that everyone experiences change and loss allows us to connect more deeply with others and to offer support and kindness. Impermanence reminds us of our shared humanity and encourages us to approach each moment with an open heart and a spirit of generosity. By embracing the wisdom of impermanence, we can live more fully, love more deeply, and create a life that is rich in meaning and connection.

6

Chapter 6: The Power of Connection

Human beings are inherently social creatures, and our connections with others are a vital source of meaning and fulfillment in our lives. The power of connection lies in our ability to empathize, to share our experiences and emotions, and to support and uplift one another. It is through our relationships that we learn about ourselves and the world and find a sense of belonging and purpose. The art of living fully involves nurturing our connections with others, cultivating empathy and compassion, and fostering a sense of community and togetherness. By building strong and meaningful relationships, we can create a supportive network that enriches our lives and helps us navigate the challenges and joys of existence. The power of connection is a testament to our shared humanity and a reminder that we are all interconnected.

At the heart of connection is the ability to listen deeply and to communicate authentically. Genuine connection requires us to be present and engaged, to listen with an open mind and heart, and to express ourselves honestly and vulnerably. By creating spaces of trust and understanding, we can build deeper and more meaningful relationships. Connection is not just about being physically present, but about being emotionally and mentally present with others, and showing up with our whole selves.

Connection also involves the practice of empathy, the ability to understand and share the feelings of another. Empathy allows us to see the world through the eyes of others, to appreciate their experiences and perspectives, and to offer support and compassion. By cultivating empathy, we can build stronger and more resilient relationships, and create a sense of community and belonging. Empathy reminds us that we are not alone, and that we are all connected by our shared humanity.

In a world that often prioritizes individualism and competition, the power of connection offers a different path, one that values collaboration, cooperation, and mutual support. By fostering a sense of connection and community, we can create a more compassionate and inclusive world. The power of connection is a reminder that we are stronger together, and that our relationships are a source of strength, joy, and fulfillment. It is through our connections with others that we find meaning and purpose in our lives, and that we are reminded of the beauty and richness of the human experience.

7

Chapter 7: The Journey Within

The journey within is an exploration of our inner landscapes, a quest to understand our thoughts, emotions, and desires. It is a journey of self-discovery and introspection, a process of peeling back the layers of our identity to uncover our true essence. The art of living fully involves taking the time to reflect on our experiences, to listen to our inner voice, and to connect with our deeper selves. By cultivating self-awareness and self-compassion, we can gain a greater understanding of our strengths and weaknesses and develop a more authentic and fulfilling life. The journey within is a lifelong process, a continuous unfolding of our inner wisdom and potential, and a reminder that the answers we seek are often found within ourselves.

Self-discovery requires a willingness to be honest and vulnerable with ourselves. It involves confronting our fears, acknowledging our limitations, and embracing our imperfections. By doing so, we create a space for growth and healing. The journey within is not about achieving perfection, but about becoming more attuned to our true selves. It is about recognizing and honoring our unique gifts and talents, and finding ways to express them in the world.

Introspection is a powerful tool for personal transformation. By taking the time to reflect on our experiences and emotions, we can gain valuable insights into our patterns of behavior and thought. This self-awareness allows us to make more intentional choices and to create a life that is aligned with our values and aspirations. The journey within is a process of continuous learning and growth, a reminder that we are always evolving and becoming more of who we are meant to be.

The journey within also involves cultivating self-compassion. It requires us to be kind and gentle with ourselves, to forgive ourselves for our mistakes, and to celebrate our successes. By practicing self-compassion, we can develop a greater sense of inner peace and well-being. The journey within is a reminder that we are worthy of love and acceptance, just as we are. It is an invitation to embrace our true selves and to live with authenticity and purpose.

8

Chapter 8: The Balance of Being and Doing

Life is a delicate balance between being and doing, between action and reflection. The art of living fully involves finding harmony between our external pursuits and our inner peace. It is about taking purposeful action, while also allowing ourselves the space to rest and recharge. By balancing our responsibilities and ambitions with moments of stillness and presence, we can create a more sustainable and fulfilling life. The balance of being and doing requires us to listen to our bodies and minds, to honor our needs and boundaries, and to cultivate a sense of inner calm and resilience. It is a practice of mindfulness and intention, a commitment to living in alignment with our values and priorities. The balance of being and doing is a reminder that true fulfillment comes from harmonizing our actions with our inner state of being.

In our fast-paced and achievement-oriented society, it can be easy to fall into the trap of constant busyness and productivity. However, the relentless pursuit of doing can lead to burnout and a sense of disconnection from our true selves. By prioritizing moments of being, we can create a more balanced and meaningful life. Being involves simply existing in the present moment, without the need to accomplish or achieve anything. It is about experiencing the fullness of life, and finding joy in the simple act of being alive.

The balance of being and doing also involves setting boundaries and making intentional choices about how we spend our time and energy. It requires us to be mindful of our limits and to prioritize self-care. By creating space for rest and rejuvenation, we can replenish our energy and enhance our overall well-being. The balance of being and doing is a practice of self-awareness and self-compassion, a reminder that we deserve to take care of ourselves and to create a life that is fulfilling and sustainable.

Ultimately, the balance of being and doing is about living in alignment with our true selves. It is about recognizing that our worth is not defined by our achievements or productivity, but by our inherent value as human beings. By embracing both the doing and the being aspects of life, we can create a harmonious and fulfilling existence. The balance of being and doing is a testament to our capacity for mindfulness and intention, and a reminder that true fulfillment comes from living in harmony with our inner selves.

9

Chapter 9: The Flow of Creativity

Creativity is the flow of our inner essence into the outer world, a process of expressing our thoughts, emotions, and ideas in unique and meaningful ways. The art of living fully involves embracing our creative potential and finding joy in the act of creation. Whether through art, music, writing, or any other form of creative expression, we can tap into a deeper sense of fulfillment and purpose. Creativity allows us to explore new possibilities, break free from routine and convention, and connect with our true selves. By nurturing our creative spirit, we can bring more beauty and inspiration into our lives and share our gifts with the world. The flow of creativity is a celebration of our individuality, a testament to our capacity for innovation and imagination, and a reminder that we are all artists of our own lives.

Creativity is not limited to the arts; it can be expressed in every aspect of our lives. From problem-solving at work to finding innovative ways to connect with loved ones, creativity infuses our daily experiences with a sense of curiosity and wonder. It encourages us to think outside the box, to challenge the status quo, and to see the world through fresh eyes. By embracing creativity, we can transform ordinary moments into extraordinary experiences and find new ways to enrich our lives.

Nurturing our creative spirit requires us to create space for exploration and play. It involves giving ourselves permission to experiment, make mistakes, and take risks. Creativity thrives in an environment of openness and curiosity, where we are free to express ourselves without fear of judgment. By fostering a mindset of creativity, we can cultivate a sense of joy and fulfillment that permeates every aspect of our lives.

The flow of creativity also involves connecting with others and sharing our creative gifts. When we collaborate with others, we can combine our unique perspectives and talents to create something truly special. Whether through teamwork at work, community projects, or simply sharing our passions with friends and family, creativity strengthens our connections and enriches our relationships. The flow of creativity is a reminder that we are all creators, and that by embracing our creative potential, we can bring more beauty and inspiration into the world.

10

Chapter 10: The Gift of Gratitude

Gratitude is the practice of recognizing and appreciating the goodness in our lives. It is a powerful tool for cultivating a positive mindset and enhancing our overall well-being. By focusing on the things we are grateful for, we can shift our perspective and find joy in the simple pleasures and everyday moments. The art of living fully involves developing a gratitude practice and making a conscious effort to acknowledge and celebrate the blessings in our lives. Gratitude helps us to cultivate a sense of abundance, to build stronger relationships, and to navigate challenges with a greater sense of resilience and hope. The gift of gratitude is a reminder that there is always something to be thankful for and that by appreciating the present moment, we can create a more fulfilling and joyful life.

A gratitude practice can take many forms, from keeping a gratitude journal to expressing appreciation to others. By regularly reflecting on the things we are grateful for, we can train our minds to focus on the positive aspects of our lives. This shift in perspective can have a profound impact on our overall well-being, reducing stress and enhancing our sense of happiness and contentment. Gratitude also helps us to build stronger and more meaningful relationships, as it encourages us to express our appreciation and to recognize the contributions of others.

Gratitude is not just about acknowledging the good times; it is also about finding meaning and growth in challenging experiences. By recognizing the lessons and opportunities that come from adversity, we can cultivate a sense of resilience and hope. Gratitude helps us to see the silver lining in difficult situations and to appreciate the strength and wisdom we gain from overcoming obstacles. It reminds us that even in the midst of hardship, there is always something to be thankful for.

The gift of gratitude is a powerful reminder that our lives are filled with blessings, both big and small. By cultivating a practice of gratitude, we can create a more positive and fulfilling life, and share that positivity with those around us. Gratitude is a celebration of the present moment, a reminder to appreciate the beauty and goodness in our lives, and a testament to the power of a thankful heart.

11

Chapter 11: The Courage to Change

Change is an inevitable part of life, and it often requires us to step out of our comfort zones and embrace the unknown. The courage to change involves facing our fears, taking risks, and trusting in our ability to adapt and grow. The art of living fully requires us to cultivate a mindset of openness and flexibility, and to see change as an opportunity for growth and transformation. By embracing change, we can discover new possibilities and create a life that is more aligned with our values and aspirations. The courage to change is a testament to our resilience and determination and a reminder that we have the power to shape our own destiny. It is a call to action, an invitation to live with intention and purpose, and to embrace the ever-changing nature of life with grace and confidence.

Change can be daunting, but it is also a powerful catalyst for personal growth. It challenges us to reevaluate our beliefs, behaviors, and goals, and to make conscious choices that align with our true selves. By approaching change with a positive and proactive attitude, we can turn uncertainty into opportunity and create a life that is rich in meaning and fulfillment. The courage to change involves trusting in our ability to navigate the unknown and to find our way through the challenges and opportunities that life presents.

Embracing change also requires a willingness to let go of what no longer serves us. This may involve releasing old habits, beliefs, or relationships that hold us back from reaching our full potential. By letting go of the past, we create space for new experiences and possibilities to enter our lives. The courage to change is about recognizing when it is time to move on and having the strength to take the necessary steps to create a better future.

Ultimately, the courage to change is a journey of self-discovery and empowerment. It is about embracing our inner strength and resilience and trusting in our ability to create a life that is aligned with our true selves. By cultivating the courage to change, we can transform our lives and create a future that is filled with possibility and purpose. The courage to change is a reminder that we have the power to shape our own destiny and that by embracing the unknown, we can create a life that is truly fulfilling.

12

Chapter 12: The Joy of Simplicity

In a world that often prioritizes busyness and accumulation, the joy of simplicity offers a refreshing and fulfilling alternative. The art of living fully involves embracing a simpler, more intentional way of life, and focusing on the things that truly matter. By decluttering our physical and mental spaces, we can create more room for joy, creativity, and connection. Simplicity allows us to appreciate the beauty of the present moment, to find contentment in the little things, and to cultivate a greater sense of peace and well-being. The joy of simplicity is a reminder that less is often more and that by simplifying our lives, we can create more space for what truly matters. It is an invitation to live with intention, to prioritize our values and relationships, and to find fulfillment in the beauty of simplicity.

Simplicity is not about deprivation or sacrifice; it is about making conscious choices that align with our values and priorities. By focusing on what truly matters, we can create a more meaningful and fulfilling life. This may involve letting go of material possessions, limiting distractions, and creating space for what brings us joy and fulfillment. The joy of simplicity is about finding contentment in the present moment and appreciating the beauty and abundance that already exist in our lives.

Simplicity also involves cultivating a sense of mindfulness and presence. By slowing down and being fully present in the moment, we can savor the simple pleasures of life and find joy in the little things. Whether it is enjoying a cup of tea, taking a walk in nature, or spending time with loved ones, simplicity allows us to appreciate the richness and beauty of our everyday experiences. The joy of simplicity is a reminder that true fulfillment comes from within and that by simplifying our lives, we can create more space for joy, creativity, and connection.

In embracing simplicity, we also cultivate a greater sense of gratitude and contentment. By focusing on what we have, rather than what we lack, we can develop a mindset of abundance and appreciation. Simplicity allows us to let go of the constant striving for more and to find contentment in the present moment. The joy of simplicity is a powerful reminder that we already have everything we need to live a fulfilling and meaningful life. It is an invitation to slow down, be present, and appreciate the beauty and abundance that exist in our lives.

13

Chapter 13: The Strength of Vulnerability

Vulnerability is often seen as a weakness, but it is, in fact, a source of great strength and authenticity. The art of living fully involves embracing our vulnerabilities and recognizing that they are an integral part of who we are. By allowing ourselves to be vulnerable, we open up to deeper connections, greater self-awareness, and more meaningful experiences. Vulnerability requires courage, as it involves exposing our true selves and facing the possibility of rejection or judgment. However, it is through this openness that we find our true strength and resilience.

Being vulnerable allows us to connect more deeply with others. When we share our fears, struggles, and imperfections, we create a space for genuine connection and empathy. Vulnerability fosters trust and intimacy, and it allows us to build stronger and more authentic relationships. By embracing our vulnerabilities, we invite others to do the same, creating a sense of mutual support and understanding.

Vulnerability also plays a crucial role in our personal growth and self-discovery. By acknowledging our weaknesses and limitations, we can gain a greater understanding of ourselves and our needs. It allows us to confront our fears and insecurities and to develop a deeper sense of self-compassion. Embracing vulnerability is a journey of self-acceptance, a recognition that we are enough just as we are.

The strength of vulnerability is a testament to our resilience and capacity for growth. It reminds us that true courage lies not in pretending to be perfect, but in embracing our imperfections and showing up as our authentic selves. By cultivating vulnerability, we can create a life that is rich in meaning and connection, and we can develop a deeper sense of inner strength and resilience.

14

Chapter 14: The Power of Purpose

Having a sense of purpose is a powerful motivator that can guide our actions and give our lives meaning. The art of living fully involves discovering our purpose and aligning our actions with our values and passions. Purpose is not something that is handed to us; it is something that we create and cultivate through our experiences, relationships, and aspirations. By finding and living our purpose, we can create a life that is fulfilling and meaningful.

Purpose gives us a sense of direction and motivation. It helps us to prioritize our time and energy, and to make decisions that are aligned with our values and goals. When we have a clear sense of purpose, we are more likely to persevere through challenges and setbacks, as we have a deeper sense of why we are doing what we are doing. Purpose provides us with a sense of fulfillment and satisfaction, as it allows us to contribute to something greater than ourselves.

Finding our purpose often involves exploring our passions, strengths, and values. It requires us to reflect on what truly matters to us and what we want to contribute to the world. Purpose is not static; it can evolve and change over time as we grow and learn. By staying open to new experiences and opportunities, we can continually refine and deepen our sense of purpose.

The power of purpose is a reminder that we have the ability to create a life that is meaningful and fulfilling. By aligning our actions with our purpose, we can create a positive impact in the world and find a deeper sense of satisfaction and joy. Purpose is a testament to our capacity for intentional and purposeful living, and it is a powerful motivator that can guide us on our journey.

15

Chapter 15: The Beauty of Compassion

Compassion is the practice of recognizing and responding to the suffering of others with empathy and kindness. It is a powerful force that can transform our relationships and our world. The art of living fully involves cultivating compassion for ourselves and others, and finding ways to make a positive impact in the lives of those around us. By practicing compassion, we can create a more loving and supportive community, and we can develop a deeper sense of connection and belonging.

Compassion begins with self-compassion, the practice of being kind and gentle with ourselves. It involves recognizing our own suffering and offering ourselves the same empathy and care that we would offer to a friend. Self-compassion helps us to build resilience and to navigate life's challenges with greater ease and grace. By practicing self-compassion, we can develop a greater sense of inner peace and well-being.

Compassion for others involves recognizing their suffering and responding with empathy and kindness. It requires us to listen deeply, to understand their experiences, and to offer support and care. Compassion allows us to build stronger and more meaningful relationships, as it fosters a sense of trust and understanding. By practicing compassion, we can create a more loving and supportive community.

The beauty of compassion is a reminder that we are all connected, and that our actions have the power to make a positive impact in the lives of others.

By cultivating compassion, we can create a ripple effect of kindness and care that extends beyond ourselves. Compassion is a testament to our shared humanity, and it is a powerful force that can transform our world.

16

Chapter 16: The Harmony of Balance

Life is a delicate balance between various aspects, such as work and leisure, personal and professional, and giving and receiving. The art of living fully involves finding harmony between these different areas of our lives and creating a sense of equilibrium that allows us to thrive. Balance is not about achieving perfection, but about making conscious choices that align with our values and priorities. By finding harmony between our responsibilities and desires, we can create a more fulfilling and sustainable life. The harmony of balance is a reminder that true fulfillment comes from integrating all aspects of our lives in a way that reflects our true selves.

Balancing different areas of our lives requires self-awareness and intention. It involves recognizing our needs and boundaries, and making choices that support our overall well-being. By prioritizing self-care and setting healthy boundaries, we can create space for rest and rejuvenation, and prevent burnout. The harmony of balance is about finding a rhythm that allows us to honor our commitments while also taking care of ourselves.

Balance also involves being present and engaged in each moment, whether at work, with family, or during leisure time. By giving our full attention to the task at hand, we can create a sense of flow and fulfillment. The harmony of balance is about being fully present in each aspect of our lives, and finding joy and meaning in the process.

Ultimately, the harmony of balance is a journey of self-discovery and self-expression. It is about creating a life that is aligned with our true selves and finding a sense of harmony between our various roles and responsibilities. By embracing the harmony of balance, we can create a life that is rich in meaning and fulfillment, and find a sense of peace and contentment in the midst of life's complexities.

17

Chapter 17: The Legacy of a Life Fully Lived

The legacy we leave behind is a testament to the lives we have touched and the impact we have made. The art of living fully involves creating a legacy that reflects our values, passions, and contributions. It is about making a positive impact in the world and leaving a lasting impression on those we encounter. By living with intention and purpose, we can create a legacy that is meaningful and enduring.

Creating a legacy involves being mindful of the choices we make and the actions we take. It requires us to consider how we want to be remembered and what we want to contribute to the world. By aligning our actions with our values and aspirations, we can create a legacy that reflects our true selves and makes a positive impact on the lives of others.

The legacy of a life fully lived is not measured by material possessions or achievements, but by the love, kindness, and wisdom we share. It is about the relationships we build, the lives we touch, and the positive impact we make in our communities. By living with compassion, generosity, and integrity, we can create a legacy that inspires and uplifts others.

Ultimately, the legacy of a life fully lived is a reflection of our true selves. It is a testament to the journey we have taken, the challenges we have overcome, and the growth we have experienced. By embracing the art of living fully, we can create a legacy that is rich in meaning and purpose, and leave a lasting impact on the world.

In "**The Unfolding Hourglass: Time, Growth, and the Art of Living Fully**," discover the profound and timeless wisdom that guides us toward a life of fulfillment and purpose. This enlightening journey unfolds through 17 thought-provoking chapters, each offering deep insights into the essence of time, the beauty of growth, and the transformative power of mindfulness.

As you delve into the pages of this book, you will learn to embrace the fleeting nature of each moment, recognizing the impermanence of life as a source of joy and gratitude. You'll explore the rich tapestry of your experiences, weaving together the triumphs and tribulations that shape your unique story. The dance of growth will inspire you to step out of your comfort zone, embrace challenges, and celebrate the continuous process of becoming your true self.

Through the art of mindfulness, you'll develop a deeper awareness of your thoughts, emotions, and sensations, finding clarity and balance in the present moment. The wisdom of impermanence will teach you to let go of attachments and expectations, cultivating resilience and adaptability in the face of change. You'll discover the power of connection, building meaningful relationships that enrich your life and foster a sense of community.

Embark on the journey within, uncovering your inner wisdom and potential, and finding harmony between being and doing. The flow of creativity will encourage you to express your unique gifts and talents, bringing beauty and inspiration into the world. With the gift of gratitude, you'll cultivate a positive mindset and appreciate the abundance in your life.

The courage to change will empower you to embrace the unknown and create a life aligned with your values and aspirations. The joy of simplicity will remind you that less is often more, allowing you to focus on what truly matters. The strength of vulnerability will reveal the power of authenticity, while the power of purpose will guide you toward a life of meaning and impact.

As you journey through the pages of this book, you'll cultivate compassion for yourself and others, creating a legacy of love and kindness. The harmony

CHAPTER 17: THE LEGACY OF A LIFE FULLY LIVED

of balance will help you integrate all aspects of your life, finding peace and fulfillment in the process. Finally, the legacy of a life fully lived will inspire you to leave a lasting impact on the world, reflecting the true essence of who you are.

"The Unfolding Hourglass" is a profound and inspiring guide to living a life of purpose, growth, and mindfulness. It is a celebration of the human spirit and a testament to the beauty and richness of the journey of life.

www.ingramcontent.com/pod-product-compliance
Lightning Source LLC
LaVergne TN
LVHW020500080526
838202LV00057B/6058